GW01402915

THE MISADVENTURES OF
MODERN RELATIONSHIPS

THE MISADVENTURES OF MODERN RELATIONSHIPS

A Light-Hearted Look

AVERY NIGHTINGALE

Creative Quill Press

CONTENTS

CHAPTER 1

Introduction

The closest thing we, as a society, can measure success up to is actually getting into the relationship itself, but our master's degrees can also offer compelling arguments for climbing the social ladder of relationships. Now, we all know the basic formula for relationships: a) the thrill of the hunt, b) the defusing of your friend circle warnings, and c) the cap and gown of gradually sliding it around to being in your head and off the market. And you know, there are also the lawsuits, the infighting, and the bankruptcy. In the end, though, they don't leave you with a couple of kids to shove together like the cathedral Lego collection you always wished your grown-up self could actually support.

When Delancy first began discussing the possibility of writing for Modern Typewriter, she asked me what I wanted our topic to be. I responded, "I don't want to write about what I know because that's really all I ever talk about. I want to write about something I don't know anything about." And that is when the idea struck. Modern relationships are, in fact, something we know very little about. You see, relationships aren't like having a useful degree or managing to put the same number of toothpaste stripes down the middle of the tube. There's no quantifiable measure of what is perceived as success in a modern relationship.

CHAPTER 2

The Evolution of Dating

Before there was Monica, there was Mary. And before Mary, there was Clarice. And before any of the currently woman-serving requests read their names and got insulted, I ask that you carry on. I am well aware that I have yet to utter the names of any men. The chosen names are random but common. Most stories of relationships are female-centric. Yet both sexes are to blame for the complicated mess known as dating. Oh, dating, how you have evolved. You started as a business meant to make sure that members of the third gender didn't have to make arrangements for themselves.

While parents have consulted astrologers to see if their children will have long prosperous lives with their predictions, matchmakers have also been peddling surefire schemes known as arranged marriage for thousands of glorious years. Boy meets girl, boy jumps over fire with girl, boy tells Vedic scriptures to girl three times and voila! Boy and girl are now married under a git-opavesham, which is for some reason spoken under a canopy.

This was how things were done. Then came westernization and freedom. Love marriages were born! Vijaya Nirmal Selvamani's songs were the equivalent of Piper Chapman and Polly Harper trying to invent a better travel luggage. Some succeeded, look at Rahul Gandhi, and some didn't, look at Rahul Gandhi's hairline. Do not fear though, the new generation has not given up. This time they use technology, more specifically, Facebook. Random friends from Kerala and Bahrain are tagged in a meme about a chicken or a baby, and common interests are created. Friendship is formed.

The friend, however, is a lot like an onion. It is not until you have reached the core that the tears come. Once friendship is established, reality of the person takes center stage and dissolves online persona. First impressions make way for personality and resume. You are now in a mid-level position of the friendship bracket, and room for escalation presents itself.

CHAPTER 3

Online Dating: Pros and Cons

Online dating is more popular than ever, and the stigma of logging on to love has vanished. Mashable magazine said in September that online dating is becoming a thing that people exclusively do because it's awesome. Begin thinking that you have to do some things on your own, participate in activities frequently in order to meet others, and just relax to the possibility of a new relationship that may develop. The cons of online dating include, but are not limited to: Costume rage, being misled, being outdone by your friend's girlfriend in the finding love department, being told that you are better on paper, whilst someone openly affects an expression in slight confusion. And as our next section shall venture into the less pretty corners of the modern love spectrum – that second example, of being misled, isn't always as spontaneous as having strangers thinking you're a cheap escapist. While the positives are significantly numerous, you will very soon realize that differently themed episodes of Neville in Paradise offer no match on the excitement that any modern date may bring.

We've all heard the timeless cliché (or at least considered that it's possible) that your one true love is the person you least expect, standing right in front of you. Yet it may not be commonly known amidst our modern world that you might just accidentally meet your soul mate while getting your morning coffee, taking the subway downtown, or simply while stopping by your local restaurant for supper. All common settings for such an affair are left ignored and deemed 'no-longer-possibly-romantic' as we attempt to make room in our lives to finding love with our peculiarly modern habits - while sitting glued to our computer screens or staring at our smartphones. Such conundrums are daily events that our parents – and ancestors with previous generations – may not have had the pleasure of discovering. In this article, we explore a variety of misadventures that have only recently developed in the modern love industry.

CHAPTER 4

Navigating the First Date

After weeks (sometimes months) of WhatsAppping/calling/ FaceTiming, texting and occasionally wishing a meteorite will fall on Earth and end the drawn torture of dating as we know it, you get to the stage of meeting the other in person. You are at the first date stage (we live, we learn, we recover or revel in the after-glow.). Being of the self-proclaimed untalented and often forced via online dating single individual, I have more than enough first dates to share snippets of their embarrassing history and usefulness, so others may not go forth headlong into the abysmal space of the first date without a small semblance of guidance.

He's coming – gas blue lighted my nose, burly built up an authoritative bawl and despite my admirable effort to suction into the 'ideal woman' (demure/victoria secret air, giggly/cute face and a slim built), nervousness from head to small toes, stated heavily on my mind. But I must survive yet another first date for the purposes of enlightenment. It's not easy to cope with chief meat in text messages and then meet the actual essence. Trepidation shares itself between you as a salty combination of 'every topic' you have never had the opportunity to speak to...shush don't bring out the overdone issues, and feeling like sitting next to stratosphere when hanging with Mr. Towering Potential. Introducing – I can tell you right now, my name didn't need to be said any more times than it took for caveat: Tallish because the tall, tall gesticulating my unquantifiable height (l'esqualer unsecret), shame to be short! still lacks in my family's crooked dynamics saved by my mum's bred feet of air.

CHAPTER 5

The Art of Texting and Messaging

But sometimes, your cell phone can save you. They can tell you aloud when your thoughts are not appropriate, like an insistent, dispassionate Helen Lovejoy. I once lent mine to a friend as we paced up and down in high and grassy-back-high-heel-appropriate-society-talk-and-silence-held-orchid-tipped-heads. As I spoke through the particulars of an unfamiliar texturized texture of a soul's tiny treble journey, my phone intermittently shimmered with red light and rang out an announcer's dulcet involuntary broadcast tones, "Don't do it! Don't do it."

Laws of attraction will always assault you with modern communication woes, and the 21st century bandit has really big and mean guns. Emails, texts, WhatsApp, Messenger... and the rules, which like the commandments of millennia past, are inscribed in pixels by unseen gods. And if you transgress, you will be cast into the fire. There is no more polite way to say, "I don't fancy you at all" than to not start a WhatsApp group that includes that person and then not write anything in there. Not even an emoji. The danger is that the spurned person tells someone who tells someone who tells someone who tells the unintentional spurner and then ignores you. The spurned is then oblivious and in complete denial that they have been cut to unseen and unheard from virtual marrow, whilst you weep team-creating tears. This is gentler though than the very public un-equity of my Proustian notebook, when in a French-written-holiday-message fumble, I told my godmother in explicit language that it was hard for me to talk to her because she barely spoke in anything other than French - and I fluffed it. Oh my guardians, governesses, I make myself blush even now, intending as I did or more appropriately, didn't, to send to a very present-parented friend. I perused my indelicacy this summer, if I could even reach the word count in Proust's notebook diary, I'd say it was huge. Or elegiac aubergine.

CHAPTER 6

Social Media and Relationships

Social media is not a good judge of relationships. Relationships happen behind closed doors, so to number them with follows and likes is futile. It can also be childish. The most arrogant person is accusing another of their like count or lack of responses, as if each notification is akin to vows or promises, so we either blame the platform or childishly boast. 'Didactic' - social media is a mess, so it's a good thing the relationships on it are false. Consider the filters, FaceTuned candids, read messages, censoring, daily occultations and angsty galore one views all over the internet in the name of 'art' - more importantly, 'insta-art'. As always, each relationship is unique (please read a book with a complete title at least once in your lifetime).

I find that disposal is a convenient trait of most modern relationships primarily due to unsavory use of the 'Block' button. Couples, friends, acquaintances, marriages - a fight leads to silence. But instead of attempting communication or resolution, many flee or postpone (which is just as dismissive), which makes not speaking a cold soak. On the other hand, because a falling out is discomforting, it is often the case that partners communicate through social media or messages (whilst blocking). If this is true then reflect upon what shallow roots so hypocritically thrive within - not to say this may be enlightening for someone else. Would it not be easier to write and then talk instead of writing that which you must not say? Only honesty and dialogue may serve as the sole alchemists trained in speaking to the depths of friendship and affection. Carelessness and block buttons will mar.

CHAPTER 7

Long-Distance Relationships: Challenges and Tips

Surprise visit. From time to time, the visit could be an occasion to communicate face to face and address directly any situation or troubles that arose between you, or maybe in your work or personal life. The idea of knowing that your partner will visit you in the end could reinforce the excitement of being patient until that wonderful moment when you will be in each other's company. Finally, write snail-mail love letters. Nowadays, the speed and ease with which we can communicate via telephone or computer can almost make us forget that, during the 19th century, lovers used to profess their feelings through written letters. Every other method is quicker, but a handwritten letter is more intimate and could act as a treasure to those involved. Of course, the letters should not be dramatic and filled with tragedies or sweet as honey; rather, they should contain words from the heart and a reflection of the feelings when being together.

In a long-distance relationship, keeping the flame alive and the relationship's aura positive could be more challenging, but the rewards are double the grand. A few tips for maintaining a solid connection during a long-distance relationship could be to establish the rules and to trust each other. Just like in any other relationship, constant communication is vital to keep the bond strong throughout the miles. Create an atmosphere of trust that would prevent jealousy and frequent quarrels, and respect each other's freedom; this way, neither one would feel caged and that their partner is breathing down their neck. Establish the rules and trust each other; this is crucial to prevent jealousy and create a peaceful atmosphere. Next, be supportive. It is good to meet in person from time to time, to address any situation or troubles, to celebrate something joyous, or to get an actual hug rather than one only through the webcam. Besides, the surprise visits or the planned ones are good practices to maintain a strong rapport.

CHAPTER 8

The Role of Communication in Modern Relationships

For some reason, necessary communication needed in a relationship can make men feel a little uncomfortable. Mainly because we live in a world where hate campaigners use Twitter like no other, grown men act like children because of balls, and police use criminal records to decide who the front man of a band will be. I'm also not convinced it is fair to blame the whole of our cumbersome male race that an inability to share feelings is important ground for divorce. It should be seen as a testament to our honesty that we only share our feelings about important matters. If a man bothers to tell you his feelings, it's because it is of vital importance or it is, at the very least, logical. Understanding allows you the means to make better decisions. Why did you pour a boiling cup of ginger tea into my bed, who scored for Norwich last night, and do I still exist because no one has looked me in the eye for four days, and if I do, am I in trouble?

Communication in a relationship is important; it's virtually all you really have to get by. It's lucky that there is always something to talk about, being as a relationship is as complicated as a rat that has somehow ingested the entire Encyclopaedia Britannica. Luckily, most of us know how to ask things like "what time is dinner?" and "why don't you love me at birthday time?" Women are all good at expressing our feelings, and men are all good at listening. On the flip side, men are terrible at expressing their feelings, and women are bad at not listening. The natural order of men involves them taking a strong personal interest in no subject ever invented, providing nothing factual could possibly be as important as keeping the details of some secret internal process to themselves.

CHAPTER 9

Dealing with Relationship Fears and Insecurities

Fear of communication and lack of skills to sail the ocean of love with candor and empathy make our lives millions of times more difficult. In today's world, we often take advantage of the low cost of emotional processing. We rarely give feedback, fearing our mutual relationships, because we discuss the error condition of the binary data. We provide cursory information, calling the dates and our trendy relationships open and frank. We fear inquiring about a person's current intentions; we collapse as if we overloaded the stack, trying to be straight when we are still learning to comprehend. As computer geeks who accidentally lovers of operas and pods of dolphins, nearly everyone is professional hypocritical dreamers longing for each other's excellence, eagerly awaiting relational perfection under the aura of an overly enthusiastic mentor.

Why are so many people complaining about the terrible plight of dating? Fear of rejection is the number one culprit, feared even more than death, mummified or uprooted trust funds. People are often afraid of becoming abused in their relationships, afraid of feeling humiliated and insulted, so we hold back our feelings in an attempt to protect ourselves and boost our fragile self-esteem and ego. We frequently misperceive our interpersonal relationships through the lens of our insecurities, defensive tactics percolating among our submerged concerns and irregular ideas about justice. Some people believe this fear of feeling vulnerable makes them appear weak, rather than making them stronger, and always on guard, we want to save ourselves from all kinds of social dangers by imagining our hypothetical situations and occasional ominous adverbial cues.

CHAPTER 10

The Impact of Technology on Intimacy

A prime example of a digital, yet intimate relationship noted above, are instant sexual encounters. In a study of university students' sexual attitudes and behaviors, some 76% of its participants reported that they used dating applications on their smartphones and 53% reported that they used mobile devices more generally to search for instant sexual meetings. Working in the online sphere, saw that cybercadres, with the aid of digital technologies, could escape dissatisfaction in their real-life relationships without confronting the partner, and their strong online alliance may lead to an affair. Yet, the partner, although suspicious, may initially be ambivalent and inactive as they accept the misinformation provided, which would occasionally facilitate a few offline sexual encounters. Social media sites have increased availability to nosy interests by other women, and for the search of impersonal relationships.

The profound human intimacy of face-to-face conversation is powerful, and yet the increasing presence of digital technology in our relationships is causing a number of challenges. Digital technology causes much of the intimacy and mutual support in relationships to be deflected to computer or device screens rather than part of face-to-face social interaction. The specific problems caused by technology include: a decrease in social network size; fewer face-to-face relationships; lower intimacy norms and lonely lives. However, our overuse of technology affects not just global, but also intimate and personal circles. Examples of these challenges are the observed impact that smartphone use has on family relationships. Smartphone users paid less attention to their companion and reported feeling less close to them than people in the other two conditions.

CHAPTER 11

Balancing Independence
and Togetherness

It's 11 PM on a Sunday night and Michel is suddenly swindled with emotions teetering on bitterness. He just realized that this blog post is about a couple of tips and he is 1000 words in with nothing ready. After consulting with some harmless activities, his goal is to use his primal instincts, dig into his first draft and just finish it, copy-paste it into WordPress, and so take a passive-aggressive tone to make a point about how easy it is to do this while not really writing anything. But then it turned out that he would not have to do that anyway because the topic was all these little things in relationships; or rather, a bunch of tired/inaccurate/bigger expressions/little philosophies/cynical punchlines. Perhaps I would have had a pretentious (i.e. delicious) discourse. A real lecture. Disgusting, it's the sort of ambiguous dance that the frustrating blend of togetherness and independence could use.

Striking the right balance between independence and togetherness is tough. On the one hand, we want to surmount our emotional dependence. You know, the sort of suffocating relationships where you feel like a little girl when you just wanted to be a woman who shares her life with a partner. On the other end of the spectrum is the other extreme: people being so independent in the way that they prioritize their life compulsively that any form of togetherness feels foreign, almost uncomfortable. "Towen," according to popular culture, is about making it work between someone whose actions are acceptable because they are engrossed in individualism, and someone who can't figure out how the other person can have opinions based on their own situation. That is quite a lot to say about not much. But you know, the culture is about taking a meaning, making it into two big vague abstract concepts and playing with the words until we pass it off as light-hearted but clever intellectualism. So, independence is put up against togetherness.

CHAPTER 12

The Influence of Friends and Family on Relationships

What do you do when you are a single person and you don't know anything about relationships but you've been invited to give your opinion when it comes to relationships? Decline.

Single people in relationships are usually itching to give out advice especially in an area where they have had some kind of experience. It's very easy to look at people in relationships and give them unsolicited advice since some impartiality is involved. Just as we measure the extent of our courage through the trials we face, people also measure the extent of their happiness based on how far they have gone after experiencing unhappiness. It's not always the best basis for people to freely give out the how-tos of relationships but since what doesn't kill us only makes us stronger, the cycling of information continues. So it's important for people in relationships to make a stand regarding the advice of their single friends (can work for unmarried couples as well) on how to sustain their relationship; however, it is also important for their single friends to remember that the burdens of relationships don't only come from within the relationship but from society and everyone else as well.

What do you do when there's something you don't really want to do in your relationship? You consult, of course. You will consult Tita who raised 4 children, or your grandmother who treated your grandfather like he's a tot every time he needed money, or your mother who threatens to get her own place every time she and her husband have an argument. That seems inappropriate, right? That's still called common sense because not doing what you want to do in a relationship can be a cause of conflict as well. That's in your best interest too.

What do you do when there's something you want in your relationship? You consult, of course. You will consult your cousin who is single, or your brother who argues with his wife all the time, or your sister who is clueless when it comes to love, or your best friend who is in an on-and-off LDR. That's called common sense.

CHAPTER 13

Maintaining Individuality
in a Relationship

Sometimes though, the change in behaviors and standards is a little more predictable. Case in point: "The Chair." Precious, indeed, but I'd take "you can wail at your own germs once you've (beep)ing in the chair" as an expression of love any day. I must admit it does make a great deal of sense and foresight too — you see, my struggle to multitask is a well-defined one. So "The Chair" and I, we reach a mutually beneficial agreement. We share the responsibilities, and in return, the goods. A bond that we have been creating ever since "It's a Girl".. The truth of the matter is, when I was growing up, I was too preoccupied with the important things in life — like shopping and screw-the-parents parties and ILP Leadership duties. Maintaining individuality in the relationship? Pschah, I got more important things to do than that.

Maintaining individuality in a relationship while still working together to build a joint future is a common approach to relationships nowadays — at least, in principle. But in practice, as partners get closer and their lives become more enmeshed, funny little things start happening. Personal grooming standards take a nosedive. Baby talk invades intimate conversations. And don't get me started on joint Facebook accounts. A hastily done, sneakily shot mobile phone snap of your beloved sleeping soundly after a bout of sinus attack is all good until "our" comments come in. "She's got more than enough Vicks on her forehead, methinks," courtesy of his boy buddy who is too rude to know that I'm 100% shoulder-rub approved.

CHAPTER 14

The Importance of Trust and Honesty

I want to relativize one thing in this text though. For those in denial or fear, for what it's worth, I am so happy for you, truly. I really am! Keep it up! After being engaged, only to be cheated on by exchanging the ring we exchanged, the relevance of trust is more apparent than ever to me. From now on, if whatever is worth, I have made sure my ducks are in a row and my honesty is spelled out very clearly from the start unequivocally. This way, the partner has the ability to make an informed decision about if he wishes to be involved. Agreeing on the boundaries early, unequivocally, and honestly, contributing over and over again, and then kissing to him casual or your but tells how the night was this with you what you told before of what you are has had concerns and how this was related to those accusations that you did make, big are assured of mutual respect. A common theme in the book's chapter is about supporting for stability.

I was speaking to a friend who expressed to me how angry she was with a guy she was seeing because he was still on Tinder and had

191 unread messages. Now, this is not to imply she was on it too or that it's exclusive nowadays, but sometimes we don't talk to those who aren't right for one another enough, and maybe she could have shown more interest and be more genuine instead of searching for other perspectives too.

It would be impossible to write about modern love and relationships without discussing the importance of trust and honesty. These concepts seem basic and very much a given, but the more people I speak to, the more apparent it becomes that these basics are often set aside when it doesn't suit or when the outcome simply justifies how the relationship has gone. This is often a form of victimization, but worse, sometimes neither people are fully honest with each other about the agreement of the rules of their relationship.

CHAPTER 15

Overcoming Relationship Obstacles

And then, there are some obstacles that make us act illogically for long enough to create an unconquerable chasm. Call me a hypocrite, but if I were to invest a significant portion of my life in a relationship, continue to invest day in and day out, and then have my partner suddenly sever it entirely, without any logical explanation, it would be easier for me to pick myself up and let go. When we are in the eye of the storm, we forget that this resilience is our saving grace; it leads to the end of relationships, but it also leads to new ones, or lets us revive the ending ones. For example, when someone hurts us, we cope with it by undergoing the usually torturous route of first taking it personally, before self-esteem and experience help us marinate pain, obscure logic, ease us astonishingly into forgiveness, leaving our well-meaning emotions, and by extension a relationship, more valuable than ever.

Not every relationship is a fairytale, and not every couple is likely to find themselves effortlessly living happily ever after. All relationships have their ups and downs, and in the heat of the moment, it can sometimes be easy to let one or two downs overshadow the ups. At such times, it's important to consider the obstacles that exist for everyone - and remember that if we are to overcome them, we need to navigate through them carefully and skillfully. This might mean cutting our partners a bit of slack - being familiar enough with a relationship obstacle to be able to navigate it without feeling insecure about the relationship. It's a delicate dance to maintain this balance; too much slack and we're dangerously close to apathy, but not enough slack and we're stifled, bearing an unconscious grudge.

CHAPTER 16

The Role of Conflict Resolution in Healthy Relationships

We will all borrow a leaf from the Misadventures of Awkward Black Girl, when the author who plays Jay confronts the awkward that comes with pointing out your partner's imperfections. When the almost perfect part that is supposed to be non-existing such that both parties actually do not feel like they have ulterior motives. Watching this episode has always reminded me of a relationship from some good years ago when in the process of communication I pointed out a "flaw" in my partner's dressing, the response was "...okay, well do you know what else I don't like about men?". It would be fair to say that this exaggeration of her was leaning walls to ice giants personality, not when we were on good terms and others spying on our interactions can be heard asking "why'd you climb the walls, talk to me"?

Conflict resolution! What my mother would describe as "meeting halfway" or in a relationship developing any other viable solution such that both parties leave feeling like their opinions were validated and each awarded a win. One would imagine that two adults who have made the cognitive (and often physical) decision to be exclusive (to one another), could be mature enough in finding a way to solve minor issues. It is often hilarious when you come across couples in an open loud argument. Keep in mind open... loud. Open because everyone around them has the privilege of processing their business and giving both parties unsolicited advice and reprimand. Loud, because if you are within 200 meters (approx) of the conflict zone it is real gunshots and threat of suicide loud. By this, I mean real fire coming out of one's emotional rear.

CHAPTER 17

Love Languages: Understanding and Expressing Affection

Words of Affirmation: These people out there are known to be great at the dirty talk, a tiny bit big mouthed, perhaps occasionally a little lacking in the follow through. But they are eternal romantics. They feel a poem coming on when a lover so much as pours coffee for them. For example, instead of abandoning it in the bathroom with the cap off, they might say, "Stunningly blue toothpaste. But not as fetching as your smile." Seriously, though, even if these lovers are praising you while you are in the hospital with a gangrenous arm, please thank them and send them home so you don't lose another arm.

The term "Love Languages" has become quite familiar of late thanks to a book by the same name. In general, it is best taken as a good-natured reference to the way each of us communicates affection, as well as how we receive it. Keep in mind that the information below is meant to be humorous and plenty of us use variations of each. The best way to figure out your own love language is to consider whether you tend to hold or fidget with your phone when enjoying time with a loved one or you actually turn them upside down when the besty sends you something so that you can be completely present. And if you are on the receiving end of the phone fidgets, if you can just laugh about it and not take it personally, that's the ticket to a great relationship!

CHAPTER 18

The Art of Compromise in Relationships

There's no such thing as fair in a relationship, it's just all about if you can live with it. So yeah, so although I don't agree on the principle of meeting halfway (which would spur the whole concept in the first place), unless both people are very stubborn or if they're both kind of laid back and would let things go, but what he's offering here isn't too bad: try to get both sides out of their heads and think of what would be fair and thoroughly discuss the rest. It makes a great exercise for communication, plus this can act as the gate to why people want things that nobody really cares for.

I'm basing my thoughts on this book which goes against something that people in relationships go through routinely, the practice of compromising and meeting halfway. Now how it's actually being proposed here is something that I strongly advise against, but to some people it might actually help them. It'll encourage people to raise the issues of [what to do in various situations] and talk about what people want. I think an important thing about compromising is it's a great skill to have, it therefore most likely depends on how one accommodates who's in a relationship, and the last thing I want is to be one of those people who would not take anything as a real compromise.

CHAPTER 19

Dating in the Digital Age: Etiquette and Boundaries

There is a chunk of people who don't take me seriously on this. "What do you mean, conversations like that can't happen through text?" So, let's clarify: within my realm of experience and in line with what I focus on, here are a few types of conversations you can't have via text. You can't effectively communicate your needs, or make individual requests with your partner, whether or not the relationship aspect translates to sexuality and/or physical contact. This is because you need to be ready to respond to that person's response. Not only are people becoming more and more prone to "wanting" what they want right now - they need it or feel they should have it, especially in the minds of a generation that has grown up with personal computers and touchscreens. Another type of conversation you can't have over text: "We need to talk..." (or "Do you have time to talk?") It's 2016 and we are lucky if the avoidant party in the relationship doesn't just ignore the "We need to talk," text, or feel beaten over the head because we're forcing them into having such a conversation with us. When did we, as a species and culture, get it in all of our minds to stop talking through hard things with one another? When did we decide that our relationships and the feelings on the line in all of this weren't worth the emotional lift it takes to open our yaps and move our bodies and take up space and put our energy into saying or hearing what we mean?

During all of that exploration and vulnerability, something happened: it became a fact so widely recognized that no one felt the need to talk about it anymore. All of our communications with one another moved into the digital realm, making even breaking up a thing that couldn't be done over a nice dinner anymore, because even that didn't warrant the time spent (or gas money) to come over and say what was on our minds. We go through breakups and ends of relationships via text message. What?

CHAPTER 20

Relationship Milestones
and Celebrations

To avoid confusing folks in terms of timeline dynamics, let us begin with the natural progression - the first date. We will sidestep all the gut-wrenching mental and emotional carnage of dating in the modern world and just zoom right to the first date, shall we? It will certainly save a lot of ink (I should be so lucky). Now, if you're of a certain age, do you even remember that first date? What music made up the soundtrack of your oh-so-brief relationship dance? Often enough that will tell you a lot about the relationship itself. Looking back, I am rather amused that some of my first dates delivered a de facto comedy act experience. Not exactly my natural habitat but anything for the sake of humor, although both of us were frequently engaged in a battle of wits with unarmed opponents. The good news? A great detente always resulted. Let's call this highlight 'Laughter is the best aphrodisiac.'

As I crossed my half-century mark, it occurred to me that my boyfriend and I had celebrated what must be a bunch of significant relationship milestones and celebrations over the past few decades.

Naturally, the term "significant" is relative and very much up for interpretation. However, I have no time for philosophical introspection, so I will opt to call them the usual relationship milestones, in my usual fashion - tongue pressed firmly into cheek. Let us embark on a brief journey through this relationship milestone wonderland, shall we?

CHAPTER 21

The Impact of Work-Life Balance on Relationships

Although in the suggested but-hurt stratum provided, there are some business owners or people who are self-employed (a bit of lazy people), and some government workers depending on the country and how contented they are with their total salary and/or condition of service. Most people act as if life is an absolutely perfect ride. But then again, if what doesn't kill you doesn't try to, you definitely must survive (by God's grace). Long distance relationships too are predominant in these times. Partners in universities of one state can be greatly encumbered if their partner decides to seek a good educational foundation in another state also, but in this context. Besides the old school letter writing and once-in-a-month weekend visitation, there are cheaper alternatives like social media networks like Facebook, Twitter, SuperBird, and WhatsApp to name a few. Virtual conversations can be live now, contrary to the 90s when we simply sent mails and hoped for good network connections to keep the line of physical intimacy between two hearts open; landfill.

Every day feels like a rush and there's just not enough time in a day to accomplish everything we want to accomplish in that particular day. Some of us start the morning absolutely disoriented and by extension unhappy because we're waking up as early as 6 or 7 am to go to work and return back home at 7:30 pm or 8:00 pm. This is absolutely the time when we need to have the most conversations and recharge with the people that matter most in our lives (our partner and children). We should be strong for everybody at work and still come back home to revere the loving embrace of our families and continue to be happy. But the reality is quite the opposite. Physically, not everybody has a perfect job that loads us with all the extra money to be able to go on holidays and vacations and leave no work pending for our return. While single people go on holidays when they want to, city to city, nation to nation, travelling. Some married people wait up to 3/4 years for when the money becomes more than enough to spend on vacations and outdoor entertainment.

CHAPTER 22

Intimacy and Physical Connection in Modern Relationships

Yet, isn't this the era when singles bond over memes and Tinder photos? Well, loving voice messages and phone calls should be enough for connecting friends or partners in different countries when they're apart, right? If "non-attached body manipulation" remains the only source of meaning in a relationship, there's little hope for us as a species rediscovering the moon in a hundred years. But honestly, if everyone wants to cuddle, can't two friends maintain a relationship outside of a couple? (As long as they're monogamous and the "second significant other" of each member supports this friendship. "Consolidation, you know," commented one of the parties). Plus - some people (I hope) have always valued friendship and care over a perspective of bonding.

For this chapter about modern relationships, you haven't really been hearing the Boss talk about intimacy and physical connection here. Who doesn't either love that stuff or at least sometimes think about the best way of not living in a world where it exists? They say that the brain is the largest sex organ, which, if we consider size rather than functionality, is a real breakthrough for the ideas of past centuries. Still, I want to talk about arms, biceps, thighs, calves, et cetera, et cetera, as well, and all the amazing things that can be done with them.

CHAPTER 23

Building a Strong Foundation: Shared Values and Goals

Shared values and goals offer a strong foundation for a healthy relationship. They can be used as a guideline when stressful times arise. Having a relationship with someone who has different personal values will make us question our own basic nature. As a result, personal development and self-persecution can be triggered by a lesser sense of individual security, forcing us to continue to control instead of just letting go. What we question most is also more like weaknesses, so a clan is formed. If previously someone was obsessed with others, now this person is finally doing it on their own. Trusted people have lied to others about betrayal. Those who were happy when you were happy now distance themselves when you have problems. Once we have freed ourselves from at least possessing all, the wife comes from having the same goal and understanding.

In the pursuit of money and/or value, most people tend to prioritize anything but their emotions. People need time to be able to get there, but modern people are often impatient and want to be able to adjust early to their circumstances. The problem is that everyone has too little money to tackle all the problems in different organizations. Take, for example, a gleaming credit card. Expanding too fast can destroy value in return. While busy with building relationships or raising children, it is impossible to buy pure love. That's when 2 becomes power.

CHAPTER 24

The Role of Intuition in Relationship Decision-Making

We suggest that intuition is particularly important in romantic relationships for two reasons: 1) by spending a large proportion of their time with one another, partners develop deep insight into their partner's personality and the dynamics of their relationship. 2) Because relationships are rooted in emotions, rational thought is often either uninformative or a hindrance when it comes to understanding relationship dynamics or managing changes in those dynamics. Our discussion in the short piece will then center on how relationships may flourish when one works in opposition to intuition, applying conscious, rational thought to mitigate cognitive biases and thereby nurture the joy and whimsy of other human beings into the deeper, more mature emotions over the course of their relationship.

Intuition plays a pivotal role in the decisions and judgments we make on a day-to-day basis, from first-date vernacular to which lucky listen tugs at a tuneful heartstring. This chapter focuses on the role of intuition in decisions within romantic relationships. The transitory nature of our sensory perceptions means that intuition is hard to pin down and study, but at a high level of abstraction, we may define intuition as decisions made without rational thought: judgments formed quickly and effortlessly from minimal data. The humble claim that one works from one's gut is an appeal to intuition. An example from Achter et al. on intimacy building in relationships describes the initial encounter of a young couple over an internet dating site. They describe how, within moments of each other's online introductions, both partners intuitively understood their affair would lead to a longer-term commitment, and chuckled to themselves at the implicit severity of a relationship built from so little information (n.b. both couples do seem to be managing just fine).

CHAPTER 25

Red Flags: Recognizing and Addressing Relationship Issues

Syncing Time: Sexually, truly dedicated to one notoriety for life mimic, missed deadlines, and long-distance bonding. If you can put yourself out there title, keep their own, you should be equipped for future, equally thoughtful and intimate emotions. Be very certain, too.

Past Sexual Conduct: Men and women can have sexual histories, although only men can do so healthily. Look instead for signs of lying, misconstrued trust, and lack of maturity. Keep keen with your health, decide how much safety should factor in, and remember that your decision is yours and yours alone. Good judgment regarding your own personal experience, too, will lead to healthier relationship conduct.

Booty Calls: Enjoyable companionship is wholly possible with booty calls. But remember to give up on changing them if that's what you initially hoped for. Trust yourself and your well-reasoned boundaries. Assert them with respect and care.

Enablers: Their well-being is considering in your happiness, and they are happiest when they give. Watch for signs to discern between atypical altruism with genuine compassion: vocal martyrdom, forced help, excessive giving to those who abuse charity. Additionally, their enabler status is no secret. Do something nice for them, like buy some flowers, give a back rub, or make time for coffee dates. You can even offer them a metaphorical coming-down from the platonic love high horse. Done out of genuine affection or maybe envy, they will appreciate your considerate efforts and you will feel better for liking, not detesting, their enthusiastic benevolence. Assuming unrealistic potential for change and effort is futile, blind, and dangerous.

Givers vs. Takers: Keep an eye on imbalance in personal benefit. If one person keeps on taking without giving back balance, they are going to wear out the other person. If you are involved in such an imbalanced relationship, you are either dating a jerk or you have a lot of personal progress to make.

In every stage of a relationship, from first meeting to long-term monogamy, blissful happiness may hit a sour note. It's not enough to simply spot red flags in a relationship; you also have to address them. It will only get worse over time. But before you think it is time to cut your losses and run, some things are worth taking care of. Some things are itching for an explanation. And some things may just be plain old misunderstandings.

CHAPTER 26

The Power of Forgiveness in Healing Relationships

Forgiving them is a way we impose our superiority over their beliefs. In a situation where a person does clearly realize that there has been a wrong committed but will not seek forgiveness, it is a very personal choice you make if you can learn to let go of the pain the wrong has brought you. Forgiveness cannot bring back the past, but it can definitely help in strengthening and healing your mind over time. It is a sign of humility and strength of character to forgive, as it shows you possess the knowledge to differentiate between faulty actions and faulty people. If not, then as the popular saying goes, "Don't let the sun go down on your wrath" is a good principle to follow. Simply sleep over it and almost guaranteed the irritation from the day before will subside with time.

Forgiveness offers us a choice; a choice to let go of the past, live in the present, and look forward to the future. We often need to forgive people who do not even realize they have done wrong. We also need to forgive people who have done wrong but rightly or wrongly feel their actions were justifiable. To forgive such people, we need to accept that they are unable to comprehend the depth to which they have infringed into our rights and values, and they may never find a need to ask for forgiveness.

CHAPTER 27

Maintaining a Healthy Self-Image in Relationships

All this leads us straight to the critical question: do we want to be happy in our relationships or do we want to prove to others that we can achieve such happiness? The key lies in our expectations. Do we expect the existential happiness a "light" relationship offers or, on the contrary, do we long for a truly special form of relationship, one which has "durable" content, depth, truth, and openness to ourselves? Our happiness depends upon the emotional availabilities of the new generation of men and women, but also on the willingness to live an authentic life in which we seek the "gods" within each of us. Having gods means accomplishing the powerful transition made by truth-seekers from our existential guilt to the authenticity of offering. It is the move from "I am not mine" to "Life may flow upon me," "I am life," "I am love," "I am light".

Do lovers feel an increased sense of dissatisfaction and unhappiness because they have created false, idealized images of each other? The question is what is a perfect lover or, better, does such a thing exist at all? In my opinion, what we call love is but a way of maintaining the image of a healthy, happy and self-fulfilled individual. The instant this image is questioned, we no longer feel happy and start experiencing acute anxiety. Discordance and betrayal all too often mean that we are weaker than our partner and have to bow to both of them and our own thoughts, and also that this cohesion with our partner means the destruction of the "utopia" of strength and victory. This new image that our loved ones (supposedly) have shows that we are not perfect, that our relationship is not healthy or easy. The most recent international studies paint a bleak image: over 80% of the time, Americans believe they spend enough time in fulfilling love relationships, as opposed to 41% of couples with conflicts or unsolvable problems and 50% who claim they don't have any problems (American Psychological Association).

CHAPTER 28

The Influence of Past Relationships on Current Ones

Or have you ever found it interesting that how each person, single or married, talks about past relationships has to do with projection? The friend who 'wished he had waited' and upbraids the one who hadn't, usually for a truly innocuous version of not waiting to get around to having a spouse. The girl speaking disparagingly of men who have no more than peripheral relationships? Unsurprisingly, she has none. I've read studies, and can now recount them, that discuss gender and social-biological differences in exactly those parameters that distinguish substance-light from workable-to-overwhelming relationships. Did anyone really think that the physicist has no thought and no ethics? Even if we define ethics as concern for the well-being of others. The first time that my cousin was heartbroken over not getting the job that he had taken to after one of those famous midnight nothings-turned-everythings posture-adopting talks with his date for the night, I was surprised mostly only by the fact that he was surprised. "But, this other relationship is going so well? Doesn't he know?" As it turns out, he, along with the rest of us, understands that it is impossible to invest all of ourselves in everything.

Have you ever dated someone about whom the following is true? You ask about a prior relationship, or lack thereof, and about midway through the conversation you find yourself hoping they are not being euphemistic about the number of previous entanglements. Shadchan or shadchanit, you are talking to or dating everyone in their thirties and not yet married, because surely anyone older than that has baggage. Right? Does anyone else shudder inwardly when the guy at the sheva brachot speaks about how he had no idea his life could be this blessed or this beautiful? Meaning, of course, that his wife is beautiful and as blessed as his life is? I mean, it's a nice thought, but isn't he also implying that being single and living life unencumbered was the good-life model to beat all others until now? And that doesn't sound kind or accurate when you come to think of it.

CHAPTER 29

The Role of Gender Dynamics in Modern Relationships

We see the often perpetuated gender dynamics in typical relationships expanding into a wide array of modern relationships. I remember once asking to split the cost of food with a male friend who was still expecting me to pay for transportation. I would like to believe that I've done away with contributing to this toxic gender role in a partnership, but that would be foolish thinking. Not only does it take a very short moment for bitterness to silently build, behaviors are tougher to combat and change. While alone time to recharge is essential, it also finds itself a melodramatic device in this era of modern relationships. We needed to establish communication with coherent understanding to cultivate respect for this and other individualistic desires.

In my previous article, I addressed the seemingly never-ending conundrum of the modern relationship. A daunting phenomenon greatly characterized by the advent of technology. This part will give a discourse on the many misguided assumptions made within the concept of modern relationships. Anecdotes are shared on typical misadventures, as well as other misadventures not typically shared. It is with the hope that those who might find themselves in similar circumstances will find comfort in this, and those who are not, well, maybe some of these can give you a good laugh.

CHAPTER 30

Exploring Different Types of Relationships

"Modern marriages": By this, I mean generally non-traditional. I have no problem with two people, three people, or even 60 living together in the same space (they did/do that in the days of Krishna). The modernity borrows heavily from the West, either as a result of economic reasons or personal choice. Again, remember that the term "Western" gets its definitions changed by citizens of different countries, meaning it can satisfy whoever uses it. I have a lot of respect for the morals of Western people actually, just don't like it when someone creates a concept based on one situation and then all of a sudden it applies to everyone else. The thing is, many people fear the stigma that would occur if two people just lived together (all shacking up and all that), so that's the first step. We make it sound rather unorthodox and put on some sort of show for the neighbors – to lead them off. That this happens among Africans is actually a lot funnier (by Africans, I mean literally everyone in all the countries on this continent).

Traditional marriages: Well, this is probably the first thing that pops into our minds when we think of romantic relationships, isn't it? The benchmark against which all other relationships are measured. Traditionalism has taken a big hit though, in some cultures – in an attempt to make sure that the love element is cemented in by the partners themselves. In others, all concepts that describe the role of gender become a lot more vivid. The only thing that would apply generally is the fact that these men and women have decided that they wanted to live together to become one unit with little difference.

There has been such a drastic shift in the spectrum of romantic relationships over the years – most of us don't even know what can be referred to as "normal" any longer. Let's put some of them in the spotlight for a change and explore some new concepts.

CHAPTER 31

The Importance of Self-Care in Relationship Success

Love yourself in the healthiest way of self-care. A healthy love for another person will not cause a person to lose their desires in any aspect of their lives. In other words, any love that presents itself at the price of one's success will not prove successful in the end. Self-care communicates, "I value my goals, desires, and interests." No one person is an ultimate answer because with self-care, others become complementary options to success. Without self-care, relationships present themselves as substitutes, which again, only adds to success. I love the concept of this point because simply loving yourself can prevent people from losing themselves to others. Do not become lost or confused with another person because relationships prove unsuccessful when one is confused or ignorant of oneself. Individuals are not meant to sacrifice who they are or what they want because of this thing called love.

Do you ever sit back and think about life in general? The evolution of relationships? Or even the paradox of relationships? If so, this is the post for you. 31 of the most thought-provoking, light-hearted misadventures of modern relationships! I have witnessed, encountered, or experienced these, and in so doing, have formulated thoughts and advice about the modern relationship experience.

CHAPTER 32

Conclusion

Did I mean this conclusion title for people to relate to it as the "End of our Time?" Far from it! I am very optimistic about our society these days and I'd like to think that our little "misadventures" in relationships are just the growing pains of a younger generation working out their values and opinions. While it's easy to depict the heart of life in a comedic light, it's no gags about it that people require and flourish under healthy and meaningful relationships. Our conversation with each other in understandings and what have you are paramount in making such healthy relationships. Having the motivator of cinematic escapades that lay just beyond "the window" in the area should bring people the very least joy or even chortles, putting them in the right direction to hold the most rich and purposeful romance and friendships in life we all deserve.

I wish hilarious moments as profound as those in "Adventures in Modern Relationships" upon you and your relationships. May your ethical duality and technological know-how, censor generals and prudes, that givers and takers, those too much in love, those too much into themselves, those perfectly happy to toss your partner's book into a pool and eager to make silly movies together of any outlooks achieve exactly what they'll always want with the ridiculous and sublime moments in your adventurous relationships! Sit back, relax, and enjoy watching experience is bliss in life!

Milton Keynes UK
Ingram Content Group UK Ltd.
UKHW040329031224
452051UK00011B/312

9 798330 607389